Pirate Poems

Selected by John Foster

First published in the United States of America in 2008 by
dingles & company
P.O. Box 508
Sea Girt, New Jersey 08750

All rights reserved. No part of this book may be reproduced in any form without written permission from the publishers, except by a reviewer who may quote brief passages in a review to be printed in a newspaper or magazine.

First Printing

Website: www.dingles.com

E-mail: info@dingles.com

Library of Congress Catalog Card No.: 2007907157

ISBN: 978-1-59646-620-3 (library binding)
978-1-59646-621-0 (paperback)

© Oxford University Press
This U.S. edition of *Pirate Poems*, originally published in English in 1991, is published by arrangement with Oxford University Press.

Acknowledgments
The editor and publisher wish to thank the following who have kindly given permission for the use of copyright material:

The Agency (London) Ltd. for Tony Bradman: "I Wish I Was a Pirate",
© Tony Bradman 1991
Eric Finney for "Pirate Chief", © Eric Finney 1991
John Foster for "Smugglers" and "The Smugglers", both © John Foster 1991
Ian Larmont for "Pirates", © Ian Larmont 1991
Wendy Larmont for "There Was an Old Pirate", © Wendy Larmont 1991
Judith Nicholls for "Pirate Song", © Judith Nicholls 1991
John Rice and John Foster for "Snip the Sneak", © John Rice and
John Foster 1991
John Rice for "Wanted: Smugglers" © John Rice 1991

Illustrations by
Korky Paul; Bucket; Dominic Mansell; Caroline Jayne Church;
Phillippe Dupasquier; Martin Ursell; Christyan Jones; Andy Cooke

Printed in China

dingles & company

I Wish I Was a Pirate

I wish I was a pirate
 with a long beard hanging down,
a sword dangling from my belt,
 my teeth all black and brown.

A parrot on my shoulder,
 a patch upon one eye,
a pirate ship to sail on,
 a pirate flag to fly.

The rolling waves would be my home,
 I'd live through many wrecks.
I'd always have the best of maps –
 the ones marked with an X!

Pirates don't have parents,
 they don't get sent to school,
they never have to take a bath,
 for them there are no rules.

Yo-ho-ho, me hearties!
 It's a pirate's life for me . . .
Pistols in my pockets,
 salt pork with my tea!

Tony Bradman

3

Pirate Chief

"I'm Blackbeard, boss of this pirate crew.
Now let's see about the rest of you . . .
Sue, you can be One Eye, my trusty mate,
and you're in charge of the portholes, Kate.
And you'll do all the cooking, Sally,
slaving away in the greasy galley.
We'll all set sail from the port of Bristol;
I'll have a sword and a pistol.
You'll all have daggers, sharp and bright,
and it's Spanish gold we're after, right?
Zoe, you're just an ordinary pirate:
You'll polish the cannon and maybe fire it.
Nazreen and Lina: You'll swab decks.
Think of islands, palm trees, treasure, wrecks!
I just can't wait to put out to sea . . ."

"That's all very well. What about me?"

"I hadn't forgotten about you, Frank.
I've got you down to walk the plank."

Eric Finney

Pirates

The Jolly Roger's flying,
and the wind is from the east
and we'll sail right down the garden
and we'll have a mighty feast.

We'll eat our pirate picnic
and we'll drink our lemonade
and we'll pretend it's pirate rum
stolen in our latest raid.

We'll chase the Spanish galleons
and we'll shoot them full of lead
and we'll bury chests of treasure
underneath the flower bed.

And then we'll hoist the mailsail
with a fresh breeze at our backs
and we should just get home again
in time to have our snacks.

Ian Larmont

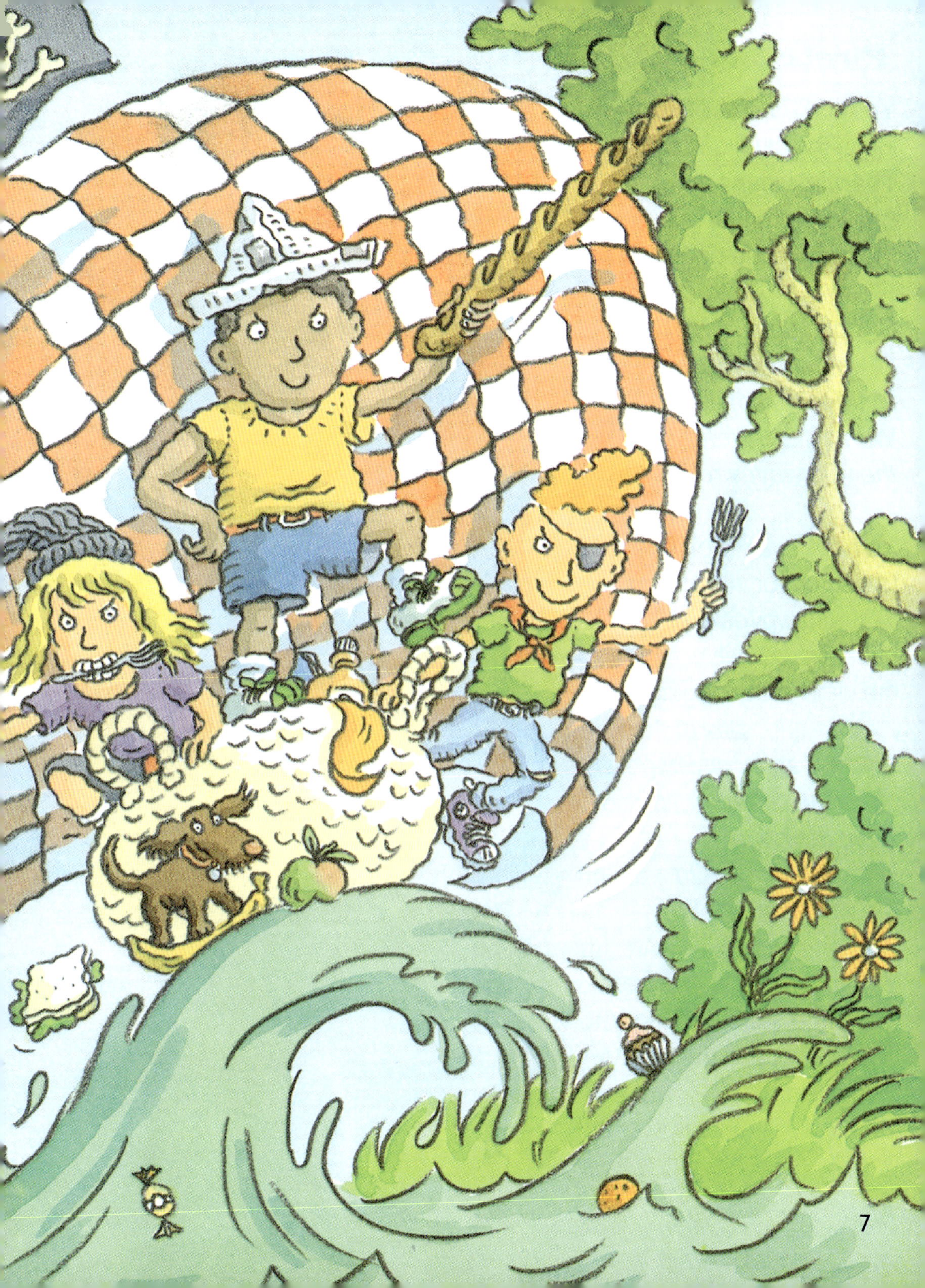

Pirate Song

Yo ho ho, we're off to sea!
Hoist the skull and bones!
The wild waves pull,
the sails are full,
the wind in the rigging moans.

Silk and satin, silver, gold;
fill up the cabins,
fill up the hold!
With a YO HO HO
the wild waves roll.

Yo ho ho, we're off to sea
to search for silk and gold!
The wild waves pull,
the sails are full,
the wind in the rigging cold.

Silk and satin, silver, gold;
fill up the cabins,
fill up the hold!
With a YO HO HO
the wild waves roll.

Yo ho ho, we're off to sea
under the stars and moon!
The wild waves pull,
the sails are full,
the wind will take us soon.

Silk and satin, silver, gold;
fill up the cabins,
fill up the hold!
With a YO HO HO
the wild waves roll.

Yo ho ho, we're off to sea,
racing under the cloud!
The wild waves pull,
the sails are full,
the wind howls long and loud.

Silk and satin, silver, gold;
fill up the cabins,
fill up the hold!
With a YO HO HO
the wild waves roll.

Yo ho ho, we're off to sea
to sail in the wild wind's roar.
The wild waves pull,
the sails are full;
may the wind blow us back to shore!

Silk and satin, silver, gold;
fill up the cabins,
fill up the hold!
With a YO HO HO
the wild waves roll.

Judith Nicholls

The Smugglers

Through the sea mist
two small boats glide,
slipping ashore
on the evening tide.

A man with a lantern
flashes a light
to warn those on shore,
"We're coming tonight."

A messenger hurries
from door to door,
whispering softly,
"They're coming ashore."

Down the cliff path
six shadows glide
to the foot of the cliff
where they crouch and hide.

They watch and wait,
not saying a word,
until the sound
of the oars is heard.

Then, quickly, they hurry
across the sand.
The barrels are passed
from hand to hand.

They are stacked in the cave
and hidden away
till it's safe to move them
another day.

Then, back to their beds
six shadows glide,
while the boats slips away
on the outgoing tide.

John Foster

Snip the Sneak

I'm reading a book about smugglers
and the exciting things they did,
about the goods that they smuggled
and the caves in which they hid.

I think I'd be a good smuggler
for I could sneak in and out.
I could sneak up and sneak down,
I could creep and crawl about.

I'm going to look in the papers
where they advertise each week.
I'm going to become a smuggler.
I'll be known as Snip the Sneak.

John Rice and John Foster

WANTED... SMUGGLERS

No experience necessary. Long trips abroad. No pets (except parrots). Excellent money to be made. Applicants must not be afraid of customs men or high waves.

Apply on parchment to
Jack "The Keg" Kingston
The Hawkhurst Gang
near the beach.

Smugglers

This morning,
while Mom was sleeping late
because it's Saturday,
my sister and I
emptied our piggy banks
and went downtown
to buy the scarf
we know she'll like.

When we got home,
my sister went in first
and kept her talking
while I smuggled the scarf upstairs
and hid it in the shoe box
under my bed.

Tonight,
we'll write the cards
we smuggled in
earlier in the week
and wrap up the scarf.

Then, in the morning,
we'll give ourselves up,
hand over the smuggled goods,
and watch Mom's face
as she opens her presents
on Mother's Day.

John Foster

There Was an Old Pirate

There was an old pirate called Pete
who captured a whole fishing fleet.
He said, "Don't be scared,
all your lives will be spared.
I only want something to eat!"

Wendy Larmont

Monster Poems

Selected by John Foster

First published in the United States of America in 2008 by
dingles & company
P.O. Box 508
Sea Girt, New Jersey 08750

All rights reserved. No part of this book may be reproduced in any form without written permission from the publishers, except by a reviewer who may quote brief passages in a review to be printed in a newspaper or magazine.

First Printing

Website: www.dingles.com

E-mail: info@dingles.com

Library of Congress Catalog Card No.: 2007907157

ISBN: 978-1-59646-620-3 (library binding)
978-1-59646-621-0 (paperback)

© Oxford University Press
This U.S. edition of *Monster Poems*, originally published in English in 1991, is published by arrangement with Oxford University Press.

Acknowledgments
The editor and publisher wish to thank the following who have kindly given permission for the use of copyright material:

The Agency (London) Ltd. for Tony Bradman: "Monsters" and "Leave the Whales Alone, Please!", both © Tony Bradman 1991
Finola Akister for "Who's Ugly?", © Finola Atkister 1991
Eric Finney for "IT", © Eric Finney 1991
Theresa Heine for "The Mermaid", © Theresa Heine 1991
Wendy Larmont for "Happynessy", © Wendy Larmont 1991
Charles Thomson for "The Lost Mermaid" and "The Sea Monster's Snack", both © Charles Thomson 1991
Clive Webster for "Mealtime", © Clive Webster 1991

Illustrations by
Paul Gibbs; Graham Round; Andy Cooke; Valerie Petrone; Dominic Mansell; Susie Jenkin-Pearce; Rachel Lockwood; Jill Newton; Jan Lewis

Printed in China

dingles & company

Monsters

Down at the bottom
of the deep blue sea
there's lots of things
that we can't see.

There might be monsters
down in the deep
that would give you nightmares,
ruin your sleep.

There might be horrors
lurking below . . .
And if there are,
I don't want to know!

Tony Bradman

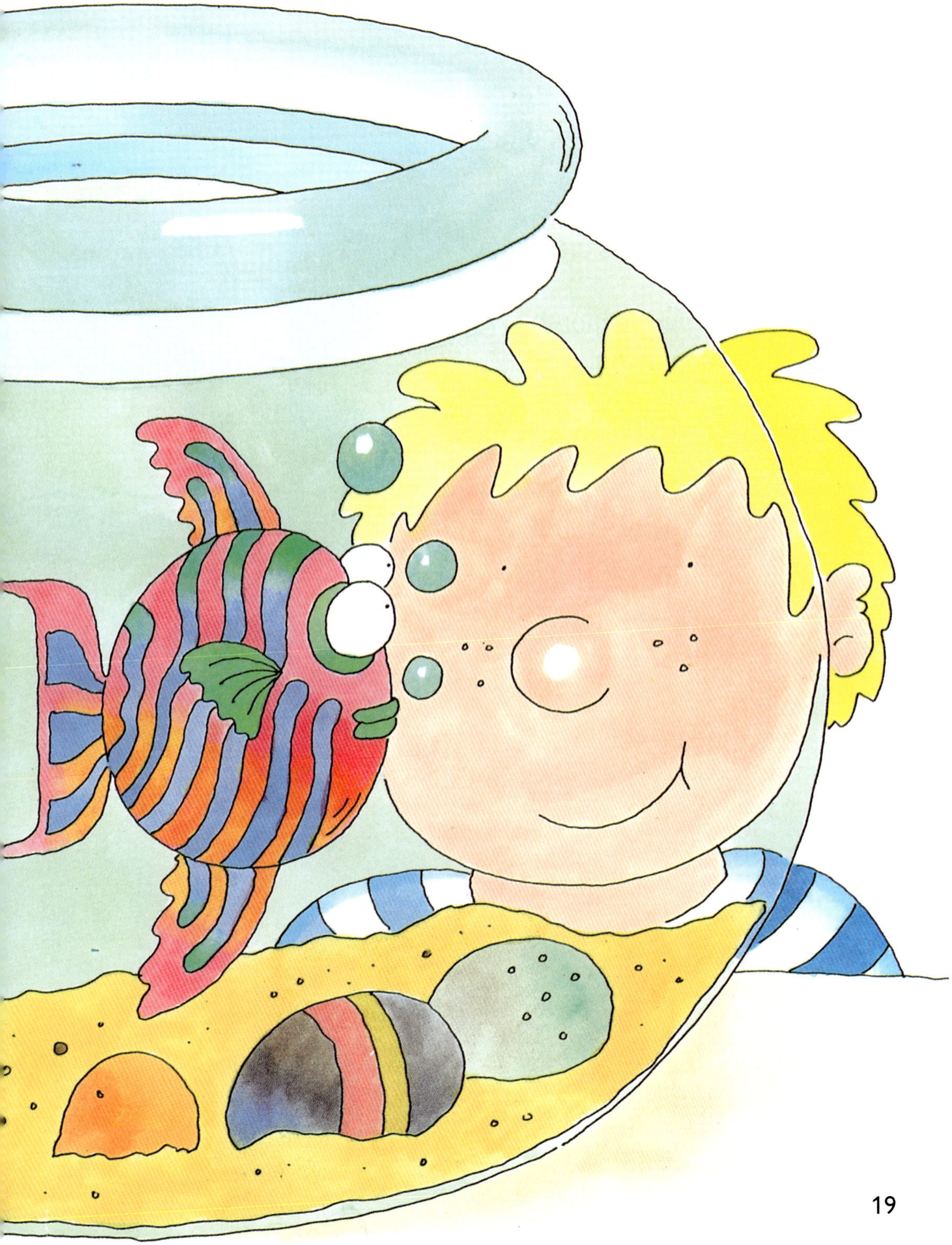

Mealtime

The octopus has got eight arms.
and I just cannot see
which ones he uses to eat food
when he sits down to tea.

Does he have four knives and forks?
It really is amusing.
I wonder how he hits his mouth –
it must be quite confusing.

Clive Webster

The Sea Serpent

A sea serpent saw a big tanker,
bit a hole in her side and then sank her.
It swallowed the crew
in a minute or two,
and then picked its teeth with the anchor.

Anonymous

The Sea Monster's Snack

Deep down upon his sandy bed
the monster turned his slimy head,
grinned and licked his salty lips
and ate another bag of ships.

Charles Thomson

Happynessy

Monster Nessy in the Loch
sleeps inside a cave of rock.
She swims around and round all day.
It seems a lonely way to play.

So when the tourists stand and stare,
she pops her head up in the air.
They gasp and take a photograph,
and monster Nessie starts to laugh.

She quickly dives and hides below.
Is she real? They'll never know!

Wendy Larmont

IT

It was huge,
it was enormous,
it came dripping from the sea;
it wobbled down the promenade,
it passed quite close to me!

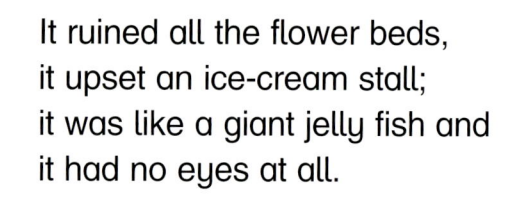

It ruined all the flower beds,
it upset an ice-cream stall;
it was like a giant jelly fish and
it had no eyes at all.

It cleared the paddling pool of kids,
its feelers swung and swayed;
it seemed to like the snack machines as
it oozed through the arcade.

It burst the turnstile on the pier as
it squeezed its green mass through.
It left a horrid track behind –
it was like a trail of glue.

It reached the pier's end railings and
it forced them till they split.
If flopped back down into the sea and
it vanished. That was it.

Eric Finney

Who's Ugly?

The monster was big, he was ugly,
he lived in the deeps of the sea.
He had three different eyes but only one ear
and a mouth where his chin ought to be.

He was covered with seaweed and shells,
but he wasn't too bothered with those.
He had twenty-two legs, twenty-two feet,
and a bump on the end of his nose.

It's quite sad to say he was made in this way,
for this monster was loving and kind.
And when fish in the sea went out for their lunch
they left him their babies to mind.

There's a moral, of course, to this story,
so remember, for what it is worth,
that your goldfish might think when you watch him
that you're the ugliest person on earth.

Finola Akister

27

Leave the Whales Alone, Please!

Leave the whales alone, please.
They don't do any wrong;
they swim in every ocean
and fill them with their songs.

Leave the whales alone, please.
Like us, they've got a brain;
but if we don't start using ours,
we won't see them again.

Leave the whales alone, please.
We need them in the seas;
we need their life and beauty,
and all they need is peace.

Leave the whales alone, please.
Let them live their lives;
let them leap, and swim, and sing —
let the whales survive!

Tony Bradman

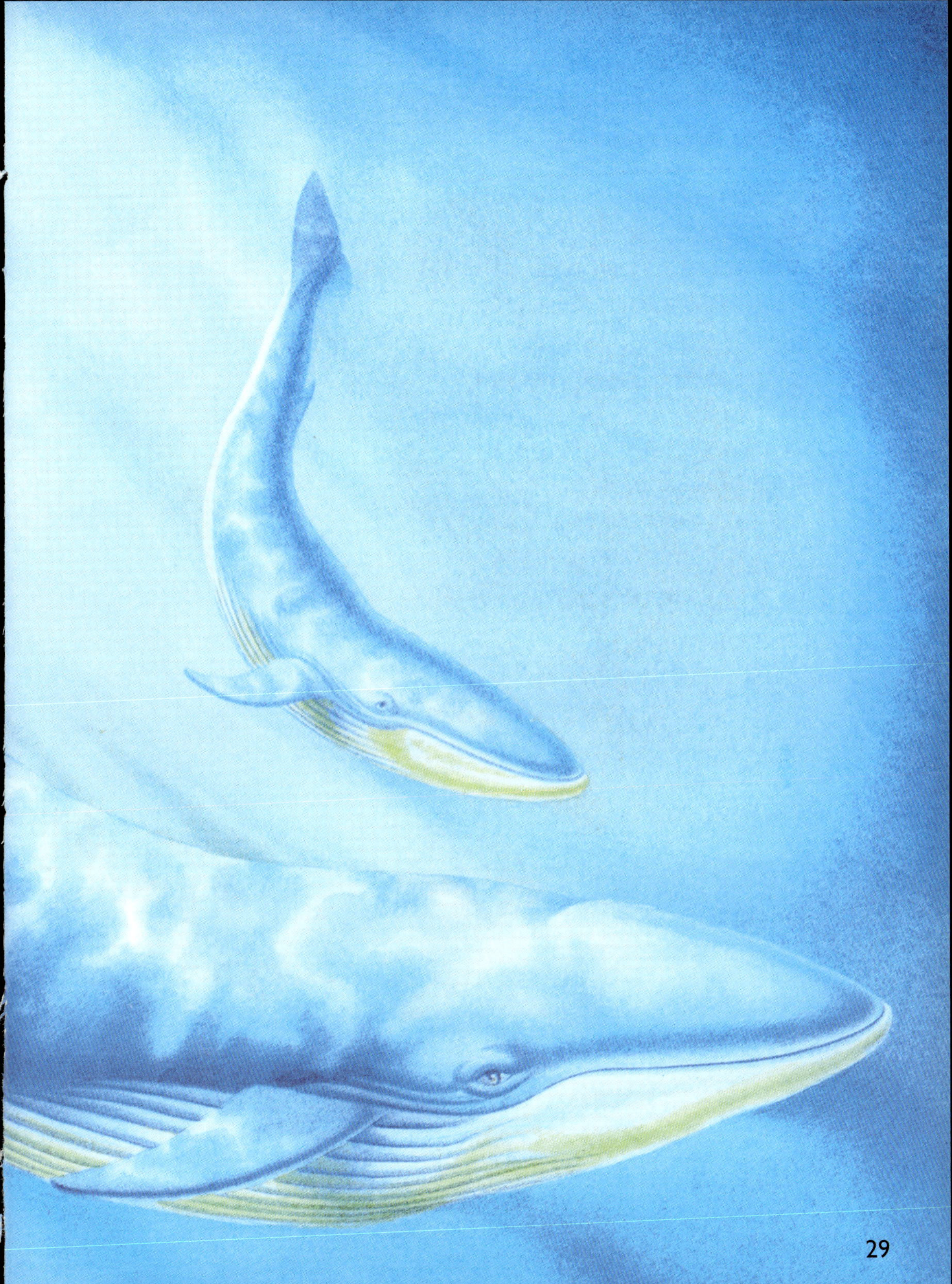

The Mermaid

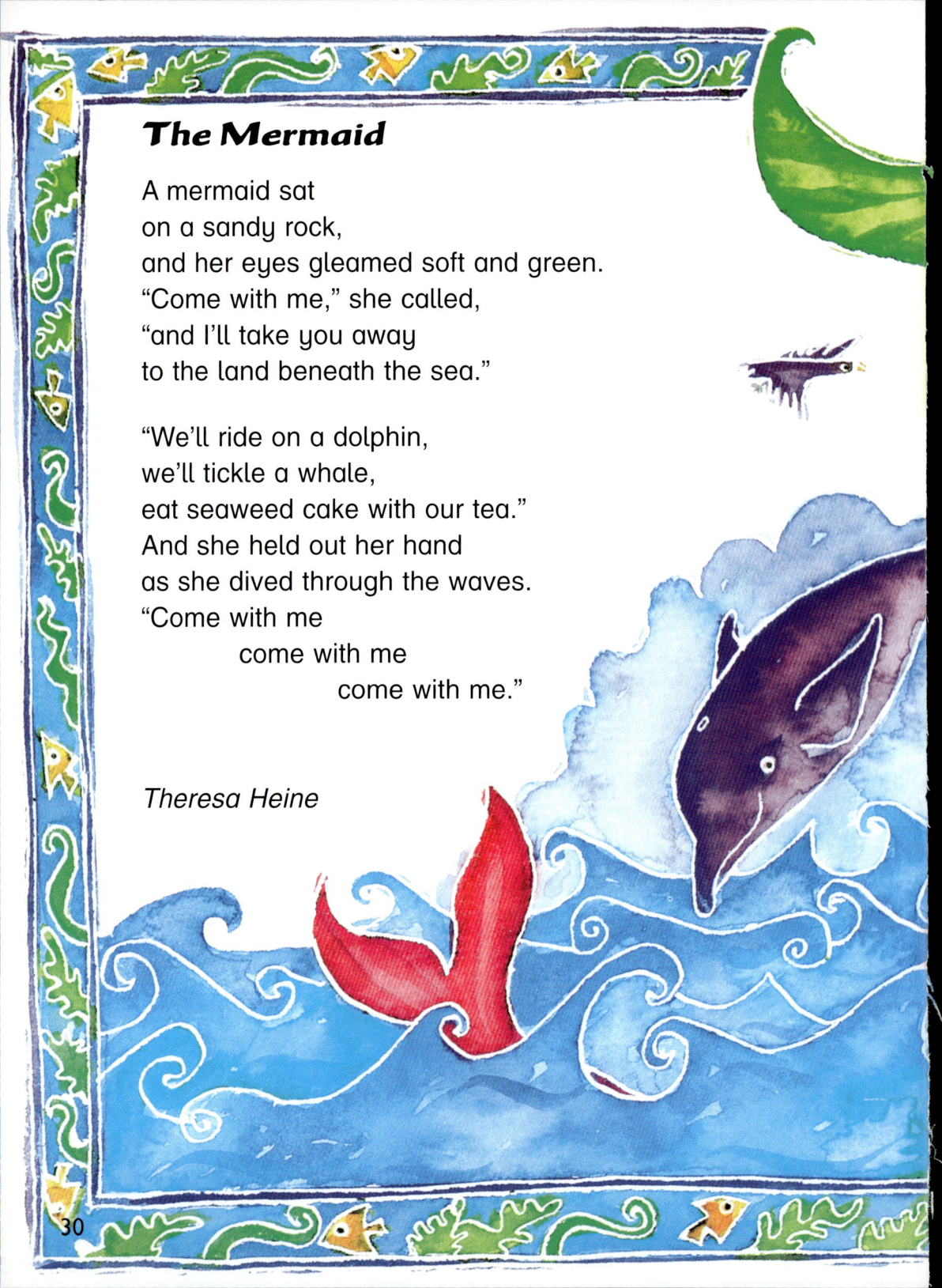

A mermaid sat
on a sandy rock,
and her eyes gleamed soft and green.
"Come with me," she called,
"and I'll take you away
to the land beneath the sea."

"We'll ride on a dolphin,
we'll tickle a whale,
eat seaweed cake with our tea."
And she held out her hand
as she dived through the waves.
"Come with me
      come with me
           come with me."

Theresa Heine

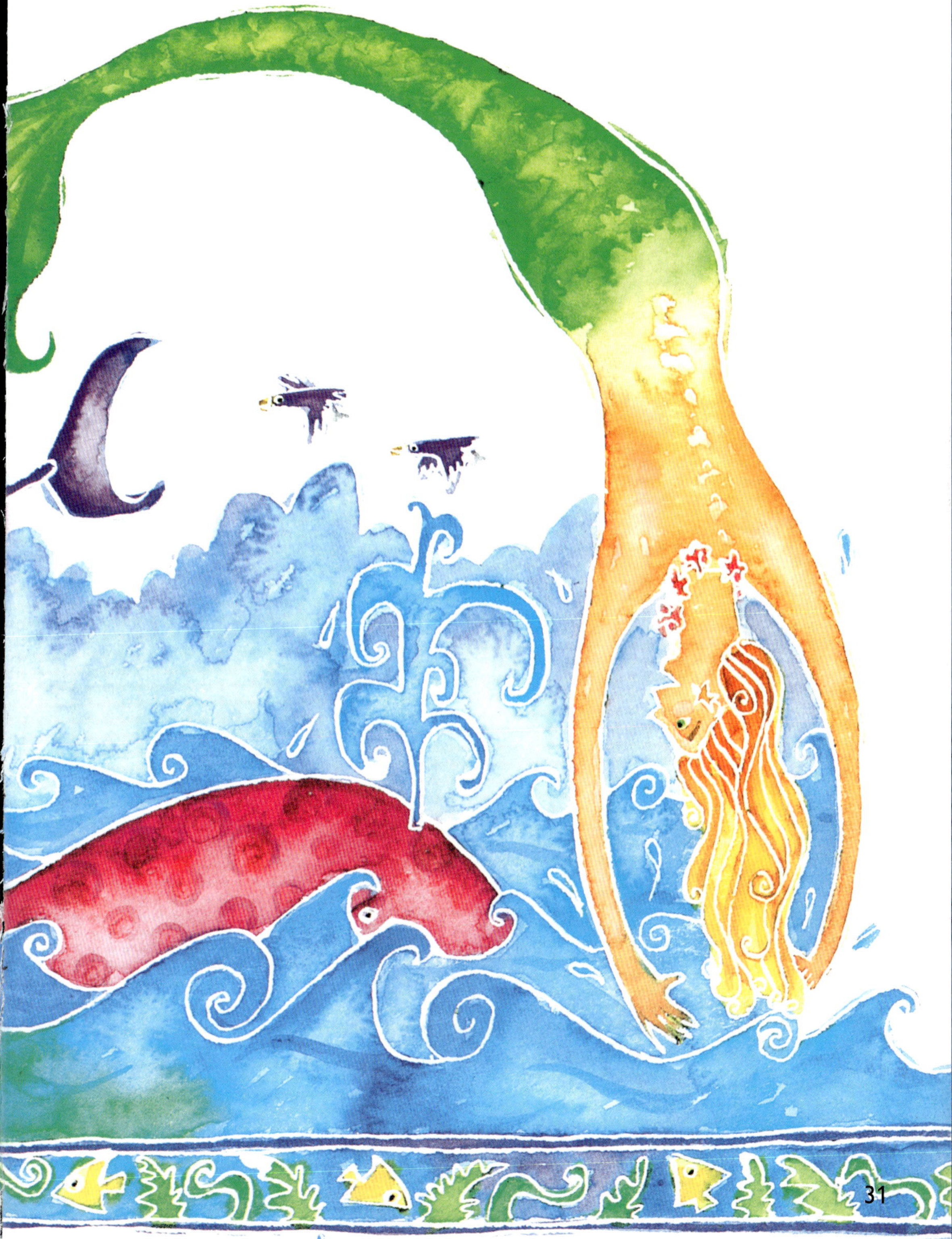

The Lost Mermaid

A mermaid came out of the drain
and said with a frown, "Excuse me,
I think I have made a wrong turn.
Is this a cave in the sea?"

Charles Thomson